THE SECRET PATH TO MOTIVATION

UNLOCKING INSPIRATION IN YOUR EVERYDAY LIFE

DR. JAGADEESH PILLAI

Made with ♥ on the Notion Press Platform
www.notionpress.com

|| Dedicated to all wisdom seekers around the world ||

ꙮ

Contents

Contents

Prayer

"Om Poornamadah Poornamidam Poornat Poornamudachyate,Poornasya Poornamaadaya Poornamevavashishyate,Om Shantih, Shantih, Shantih"

The literal interpretation of this mantra is: That which is Absolute, This which is Absolute, Absolute arises from Absolute, If Absolute is removed from Absolute, Absolute remains

OM Peace, Peace, Peace.

About The Author

Dr. Jagadeesh Pillai is a renowned Guinness World Record holder, writer, and researcher hailing from Varanasi, also known as the abode of Lord Shiva. With a Ph.D. in Vedic Science and a range of creative ideas and achievements, he is a true polymath. He is the author of more than 100 books including Research Publications. Although his roots can be traced back to Kerala, the people of Varanasi hold him in high regard and affectionately consider him one of their own.

Dr. Pillai has achieved four Guinness World Records in the following subjects:

"Script to Screen" - In this record, Dr. Pillai produced and directed an animation film within the shortest time possible, breaking the previous record set by Canadians. He has also received numerous national and international awards and recognitions for this achievement.

Longest Line of Postcards - For this record, Dr. Pillai created a line of 16,300 postcards on the occasion of the 163rd anniversary of Indian Postal Day. The event also included a questionnaire about the Indian flag.

Largest Poster Awareness Campaign - Dr. Pillai designed an awareness campaign on the subject of "Beti Bachao - Beti Padhao" (Save the Girl Child - Educate the Girl Child) to achieve this record.

Largest Envelope - In tribute to the Indian Prime Minister's

"Make in India" initiative, Dr. Pillai created a 4000 square meter envelope using waste paper to achieve this record.

Attempted - **70000 Candles on a 210 kg Cake** - To celebrate the 70th Indian Independence Day, Dr. Pillai attempted to light 70,000 candles on a 210 kg cake, which was recorded in World Records India.

Attempted - **Documentary on Dhamek Stupa of Sarnath in 17 Languages** - Dr. Pillai attempted to create a documentary on the Dhamek Stupa of Sarnath, dubbing it in 17 different languages. The result of this attempt is currently awaiting confirmation from the Guinness World Records.

Dr. Pillai is skilled in teaching the Bhagavad Gita, a Hindu scripture, and is popular among young people. He has helped many young people improve their lives through his motivational teachings.

In addition to teaching, he has composed and sung numerous Sanskrit Bhajans and patriotic songs.

He has also written and directed several short films and documentaries for awareness campaigns, and has volunteered with the police in both UP and Kerala to spread awareness about various issues through videos and photography.

Incredibly, he has produced and directed over 100 documentaries about the city of Varanasi, all on his own.

He has also helped and guided more than 25 boys and girls to achieve world records through creative and innovative methods. He is a multifaceted person who uses his intellect and the blessings given to him by God to excel in various areas. He is both a teacher and a student, always learning and teaching, and is able to master any subject he comes across.

He is a selfless social activist and motivational speaker who has overcome struggles and failures to become a successful and enthusiastic individual with a rich life experience.

In addition to his work with the Bhagavad Gita, he is also an efficient Tarot card reader, Astro-Vastu consultant, and a talented singer and composer. He has sung the entire Ram Charita Manas and Bhagavad Gita in his own compositions and has sung the phrase "Lokah Samastha Sukhino Bhavantu" in 50 different languages. He is currently working on a detailed and scientific study of Vedas, Upanishads, Puranas, and the Bhagavad Gita. He has also composed and sung the Hanuman Chalisa and Gayatri Mantra in 108 and 1008 different compositions, respectively.

Awards - Four Times Guinness World Records, Winner of Mahatma Gandhi Vishwa Shanti Puraskar, Mahatma Gandhi Global Peace Ambassador, Kashi Ratna Award, Dr. APJ Abdul Kalam Motivational Person of the Year 2017, Mother Teresa Award, Indira Gandhi Priyadarshini Award, Bharat Vikas Ratna Award, Udyog Ratna Award, Vigyan Prasar Award, Poorvanchal Ratn Samman.

Preface

Everyone has moments where motivation is low, and inspiration is hard to find. It can be easy to feel stuck and without purpose, and it can be difficult to get back on track. In this book, The Secret Path to Motivation: Unlocking Inspiration in Your Everyday Life, I explore the importance of motivation and the steps you can take to unlock inspiration in your everyday life.

The book offers practical advice for creating a sense of purpose and motivation in your life, from identifying your values and setting goals to taking action and recognizing progress. Additionally, I explore the benefits of taking action, building a positive mindset, and connecting with your passions. I also discuss the importance of celebrating successes and learning from failures.

This book is aimed at those who are looking to find greater meaning and motivation in their life. Whether you're looking for inspiration to start a new project or the courage to make a big change, this book will provide the guidance and support you need.

My hope is that this book will help you to find the motivation you need to live a life of purpose and fulfillment. I believe that everyone has the potential to unlock inspiration in their everyday life, and I hope that this book will help you to do just that.

Thank you for taking the time to read this book. I hope that you find the guidance and support you need to unlock inspiration in your everyday life.

I

Understanding Motivation - Exploring the definition of motivation and its role in achieving success

Motivation is the driving force behind our actions and the desire to achieve our goals. It is what propels us to take action and push through challenges to reach success. Understanding motivation is crucial for achieving our goals and living a fulfilling life.

Motivation can be divided into two types: intrinsic and extrinsic. Intrinsic motivation is driven by internal factors such as personal interest or enjoyment, while extrinsic motivation is driven by external factors such as rewards or incentives. Both types of motivation play a role in achieving success, but intrinsic motivation is often considered to be more powerful and sustainable in the long-term.

The role of motivation in achieving success is undeniable. It is the driving force behind taking action and pushing through obstacles. Without motivation, it is easy to become stagnant and give up on our goals. On the other hand, when we are motivated, we are more likely to persist in the face of challenges and ultimately reach success.

There are many different factors that can influence motivation, such as setting clear and achievable goals, having a sense of purpose, and surrounding ourselves with supportive people. It is important to identify what motivates us as individuals, and to create an environment that supports and nurtures our motivation.

One of the best ways to stay motivated is to focus on the progress you have made and the small wins along the way. Celebrate every small win, it will give you the boost of motivation you need to keep going.

It's also important to remember that motivation can fluctuate, and it is normal to have moments of low motivation. It is important to learn how to cope with these moments and to find strategies to get back on track. This can include things like setting new and exciting goals, surrounding ourselves with positive people, or taking a break to recharge.

Understanding motivation and its role in achieving success is crucial for reaching our goals and living a fulfilling life. It is important to identify what motivates us as individuals and create an environment that supports and nurtures our motivation. Remember to celebrate every small win and to learn how to cope with moments of low motivation. With the right mindset and strategies in place, we can achieve success and live our best lives.

"You are never too old to set another goal or to dream a new dream."

ꕥ

II

Identifying Your Goals - Learning to identify and set achievable goals

Setting goals is an essential step in achieving success and living a fulfilling life. Goals give us direction and purpose and provide us with a roadmap for achieving our desired outcomes. However, setting goals is not always easy, and it is important to learn how to identify and set achievable goals that align with our values and aspirations.

The first step in identifying your goals is to take the time to reflect on what is truly important to you. This may include things like your career, relationships, health, and personal growth. Once you have a clear understanding of what is important to you, you can begin to set specific, measurable, achievable, relevant, and time-bound (SMART) goals.

SMART goals are goals that are specific, measurable, achievable, relevant and time-bound. This means that they are clear, quantifiable, and achievable within a specific timeframe. For example, instead of setting a goal to "lose weight," a SMART goal would be to "lose 10 pounds in 3 months by eating healthier and exercising regularly."

When setting goals, it is also important to consider the resources and support that you have available to you. It is important to set realistic and achievable goals that align with your current resources and capabilities.

It’s also important to have a plan of action to reach your goals. Break down your big goal into smaller, manageable steps and set deadlines for each step. This will make it easier to stay on track and make progress towards your goal.

It’s also important to be flexible and to adjust your goals as needed. Life can be unpredictable, and it’s possible that circumstances may change and your goals may need to be adjusted accordingly.

Yes, setting goals is an essential step in achieving success and living a fulfilling life. It is important to learn how to identify and set SMART goals that align with our values and aspirations, and that is

achievable within our current resources and capabilities. With a clear direction and a plan of action, we can work towards achieving our goals and living our best lives.

"The more you know yourself, the less you are prone to making ethical mistakes."
- J.C. Watts

III

Overcoming Challenges - Learning how to overcome obstacles

Obstacles and challenges are a natural part of life, and they can often stand in the way of achieving our goals. However, it is important to remember that these obstacles can also be opportunities for growth and personal development. By learning how to overcome these obstacles, we can move closer to achieving our goals and living our best lives.

The first step in overcoming obstacles is to identify and understand them. This may involve taking a step back and looking at the problem objectively and breaking it down into smaller, manageable parts. It's also important to identify the root cause of the problem, as it will help you come up with a effective solution.

IV

Developing Self-Awareness - Strategies for developing self-awareness

Self-awareness is the ability to understand and recognize our own thoughts, feelings, and actions. It is the foundation for personal growth and development, and it is essential for achieving our goals and living a fulfilling life. Developing self-awareness can help us understand our strengths and weaknesses, and make better decisions that align with our values and aspirations.

One of the most effective strategies for developing self-awareness is to keep a journal. Writing down your thoughts, feelings, and experiences can help you understand your emotions and reactions to different situations. It can also help you identify patterns and triggers that may be impacting your behavior.

Meditation and mindfulness are other effective strategies for developing self-awareness. These practices can help you become more present and aware of your thoughts, feelings, and physical sensations. They can also help you develop a greater understanding of your emotions, and learn how to manage them more effectively.

Another strategy for developing self-awareness is to seek feedback from others. This can include asking for honest feedback from friends, family, or a therapist, or seeking out a mentor or coach. It's also important to be open to constructive criticism and to use it to learn and grow.

It's also important to take time for self-reflection. Reflect on your experiences and take time to think about what you've learned and what you could do differently in the future.

Developing self-awareness is essential for achieving our goals and living a fulfilling life. Keeping a journal, practicing meditation and mindfulness, seeking feedback from others, and taking time for self-reflection are effective strategies for developing self-awareness. By understanding our thoughts, feelings, and actions, we can make better decisions that align with our values and aspirations.

"Happiness is not something ready-made. It comes from your own actions."
- Dalai Lama

ঌ

V

Finding Your Purpose - Understanding the importance of finding your purpose

Finding your purpose in life is a crucial step in living a fulfilling and meaningful life. It is the driving force behind our actions and the foundation for personal growth and development. Your purpose is the reason you get up in the morning and the guiding principle for the choices you make. It gives you direction and helps you prioritize your goals and values.

One of the best ways to find your purpose is to take the time to reflect on what is truly important to you. This may include things like your career, relationships, health, and personal growth. It's also important to consider your strengths, passions, and values when trying to identify your purpose.

Another way to find your purpose is to think about what you would do if you had all the time and resources in the world. What would you want to accomplish? What kind of impact would you want to make on the world? These questions can help you identify your purpose and find your passion.

It's also important to understand that your purpose may change over time, and that's okay. As you grow and change, your interests and priorities may shift, and it's important to be open to new opportunities and new ways of thinking.

It's also important to remember that finding your purpose is a journey, not a destination. It's an ongoing process and it may take time to find what you're looking for. Keep exploring, experimenting and learning.

Finding your purpose is essential for living a fulfilling and meaningful life. It gives you direction and helps you prioritize your goals and values. Finding your purpose can be a process that takes time, but it is worth the effort. Reflect on what is truly important to you, consider your strengths, passions, and values, and be open to new opportunities and new ways of thinking.

"The purpose of our lives is to be happy."
- Dalai Lama

VI

Understanding The Benefits Of Mindfulness And How To Practice It

Mindfulness is the practice of being present and fully engaged in the current moment. It involves paying attention to your thoughts, feelings, and physical sensations in a non-judgmental way. Mindfulness has been shown to have many benefits, including reducing stress, improving mental and physical health, and increasing overall well-being.

One of the simplest and most effective ways to practice mindfulness is through meditation. This can involve sitting in a comfortable position, focusing on your breath, and bringing your attention back to your breath when your mind wanders. You can start with a few minutes of meditation daily, and gradually increase the time as you become more comfortable.

Mindfulness can also be practiced in your daily activities. This can include things like being present during meals, paying attention to your surroundings while walking or driving, and taking a few minutes to pause and breathe during the day.

Another way to practice mindfulness is through yoga or tai chi, which combines physical movement with mindfulness and breathing exercises.

It's also important to remember that mindfulness is a skill that needs to be practiced regularly in order to see the benefits. It's important to make time for mindfulness practice and to integrate it into your daily routine.

Mindfulness is the practice of being present and fully engaged in the current moment. It has many benefits, including reducing stress, improving mental and physical health, and increasing overall well-being. Mindfulness can be practiced through meditation, daily activities, yoga or tai chi, and it's important to make time for mindfulness practice and to integrate it into your daily routine.

"The greatest glory in living lies not in never falling, but in rising every time we fall."
- Nelson Mandela

ꝏ

VII

Understanding the Power of Positive Thinking - Exploring the power of positive thinking

Positive thinking is the practice of focusing on the good in any situation and maintaining a hopeful and optimistic outlook. It is a powerful tool for improving mental and emotional well-being and can have a profound impact on our lives

Positive thinking can help us to develop a more resilient mindset and to bounce back from difficult situations. It can also help us to maintain a more positive outlook on life, which can lead to greater success in both our personal and professional lives. When we focus on the positive aspects of a situation, we are more likely to find solutions to problems and to develop a more proactive attitude.

One of the simplest ways to practice positive thinking is to make a habit of focusing on the good in any situation. This can include things like finding the silver lining in a difficult situation, looking for the best in others, and practicing gratitude.

Another way to practice positive thinking is through visualization. Visualizing yourself achieving your goals, or having positive experiences, can help to increase motivation and positivity.

Positive affirmations are also a powerful tool for promoting positive thinking. These are positive statements that you repeat to yourself on a regular basis, they can help to shift your mindset and focus towards the positive.

It's important to remember that positive thinking is a skill that needs to be practiced regularly in order to see the benefits. It's important to make time for positive thinking practice and to integrate it into your daily routine.

Positive thinking is the practice of focusing on the good in any situation and maintaining a hopeful and optimistic outlook. It is a powerful tool for improving mental and emotional well-being and can have a profound career ahead.

"The best way to predict your future is to create it."
- Abraham Lincoln

VIII

Taking Action - Developing an action plan and taking steps towards success

Taking action is an important step in achieving success and unlocking motivation in your everyday life. Developing an action plan and taking steps towards success can help you to create a sense of purpose and motivation, even in the face of challenges. In this chapter, we'll explore how to create an action plan, determine what steps you can take to reach your goals, and identify the benefits of taking action.

When creating an action plan, it's important to break down your goals into smaller, more manageable steps. This will help you to focus on one task at a time and make it easier to stay motivated. Additionally, it's important to set realistic expectations and timelines for each step. It's also important to make sure that the steps you take are aligned with your values and life purpose.

Once you've created an action plan, it's important to take action and start working towards your goals. Taking action is a great way to stay motivated and focused on your goals. Additionally, taking action can help you to connect with your values and gain a sense of purpose. Action is also the best way to learn and grow; by taking steps towards success, you can gain valuable experience and insight into your goals.

Finally, it's important to recognize the progress you've made and celebrate your successes. Taking the time to celebrate your successes is a great way to stay motivated and recognize the progress you've made. It's also important to remember that failure is a part of success and recognize the lessons you can learn from it.

Taking action is an essential step in achieving success and unlocking motivation in your everyday life. Developing an action plan and taking steps towards success can help you to create a sense of purpose and motivation, even in the face of challenges. Taking action can help you to stay focused and motivated, connect with your values, and gain valuable experience and insight into your goals. Additionally, it's important to recognize the progress you've made and celebrate your successes. By taking action and creating an action plan, you can take steps towards success and unlock motivation in your everyday life.

"The only limit to our realization of tomorrow will be our doubts of today."
- Franklin D. Roosevelt

ꙮ

IX

Finding Inspiration - Learning where to find inspiration and how to use it

Inspiration is the spark that ignites our creativity and drives us to achieve our goals. It is an essential part of personal growth and development, and it is important to learn where to find inspiration and how to use it effectively.

One of the best ways to find inspiration is to surround yourself with positive and inspiring people. This can include friends, family, mentors, or role models who have achieved success in their own lives. They can provide guidance, support, and inspiration as you work towards your own goals.

Another way to find inspiration is to expose yourself to

new experiences, perspectives, and ideas. This can include things like traveling to new places, trying new activities, or reading books and articles on different subjects.

Also, it's important to take time to connect with nature, whether it's a walk in the park or a hike in the mountains. Nature has a way of calming the mind and providing inspiration.

It's also important to find inspiration in your own passions and interests. When you're doing something you're truly passionate about, it's easy to feel inspired and motivated.

Inspiration is an essential part of personal growth and development. It can be found by surrounding yourself with positive and inspiring people, exposing yourself to new experiences, perspectives, and ideas, connecting with nature, and finding inspiration in your own passions and interests. It's important to make time for finding inspiration and to use it effectively to help achieve your goals.

"Positive anything is better than negative nothing."
- Elbert Hubbard

ꕥ

sense of accomplishment.

Another way to build self-confidence is to practice self-care. This can include things like getting enough sleep, exercising, eating well, and taking care of your mental and emotional well-being. When we take care of ourselves, we feel better, and when we feel better, we tend to be more confident.

Positive affirmations can also be a powerful tool for building self-confidence. Repeat positive statements about yourself, such as "I am capable," "I am worthy," and "I am confident."

It's also important to challenge negative thoughts and beliefs. Negative thoughts and beliefs can hold us back and limit our potential. Recognize them, and challenge them with evidence that contradicts them.

Self-confidence is essential for achieving our goals, facing challenges, and living a fulfilling life. It is something that can be developed and strengthened over time. Setting and achieving small goals, practicing self-care, using positive affirmations and challenging negative thoughts and beliefs can help to build self-confidence. Remember that building self-confidence takes time and effort, but it is worth it in the end.

"When one door of happiness closes, another opens, but often we look so long at the closed door that we do not see the one that has been opened for us."
- Helen Keller

XI

Celebrating Your Successes - Learning how to celebrate your successes

Celebrating your successes is an important part of personal growth and development. It helps to acknowledge the hard work and effort you have put in, and to recognize your achievements. It also helps to boost motivation and self-confidence, and it is essential for maintaining a positive outlook on life.

One of the best ways to celebrate your successes is to take the time to reflect on them. Reflect on what you have achieved, what you have learned, and what you are proud of. This can be done through journaling, talking to a friend or loved one, or even just taking a few minutes to yourself to think about your successes.

Another way to celebrate your successes is to treat yourself. This can include things like buying yourself a small gift, taking a day off, or indulging in your favorite activity. It's also important to remember that celebration doesn't have to be extravagant, it can be as simple as taking a walk or a bath.

It's also important to share your successes with others. Share your achievements with friends, family, and colleagues, and accept their congratulations and support.

Celebrating your successes is an important part of personal growth and development. It helps to acknowledge the hard work and effort you have put in, and to recognize your achievements. Reflect on your successes, treat yourself, and share your achievements with others. It's also important to remember that celebration doesn't have to be extravagant, it can be as simple as taking a walk or a bath. Remember to celebrate your successes, no matter how big or small they may be, they all deserve to be acknowledged and celebrated.

"The only way to do great work is to love what you do."
- Steve Jobs

ꕥ

Other Books Of The Author

1. The Moments When I Met God
2. Kashiyile Theertha Pathangal
3. GURU GYAN VANI
4. Abhiprerak Gita
5. ASSI SE JAIN GHAT TAK
6. Hopelessness of Arjuna
7. The Soul and It's True Nature
8. Sense of Action (Karma)
9. Action through Wisdom
10. Action through Wisdom
11. THEORY AND PRACTICAL OF EVERY ACTION
12. LOGICAL UNDERSTANDING OF THE SUPREME
13. THE IMPERISHABLE SUPREME
14. Yatra Nishadraj se Hanuman Ghat Tak
15. Yatra Karnatak Ghat se Raja Ghat Tak
16. Yatra Pandey Ghat se Prayagraj Ghat Tak
17. Yatra Ranjendra Prasad Ghat se Dattatreya Ghat Tak
18. YaatraSindhiya Ghat se Gwaliar Ghat Tak
19. Yatra Mangala Gauri Ghat se Hanuman Gadhi Ghat Tak
20. Yatra Gaay Ghat Se Nishad Ghat Tak
21. MAA GANGA, GHATEN EVM UTSAV
22. Ganga Arti Dev Deepavali evam Any Utsav
23. Potentials of Digitalized India
24. VEDIC CONSCIOUSNESS
25. A Brief Introduction to Vedic Science
26. Kashi ke Barah Jyotirling
27. IMPACT OF MOTIVATION
28. Let's have a Milky Way Journey
29. Color Therapy in a Nutshell

30. Rigveda in a Nutshell
31. Yajurveda in a Nutshell
32. Samveda in a Nutshell
33. Atharva Veda in a Nutshell
34. Ayushman Bhava - Ayurveda
35. Srimad Bhagavad Gita and Upanishad Connection
36. Srimad Bhagavad Gita - an attempt to summarize each chapter.
37. Facts and Impact of Nakshatra
38. Astro Gems - NAVARATNA
39. Ekadashi - A Concise Overview
40. A Concise View of Hanuman Chalisa
41. Inspirational Gita
42. Nakshatraranyam
43. Summary of 18 Mahapuranas
44. Synopsis of 18 Upa Puranas
45. Rigvediya Upanishads
46. Shukla Yajurvediya Upanishads
47. Krishna Yajurvediya Upanishads
48. Samavediya Upanishads
49. Atharvavediya Upanishads
50. The Seven Great Sages
51. From Rocket Scientist to President Dr. APJ Abdul Kalam
52. The Visionary's Voice - Quotes of Dr. APJ Abdul Kalam
53. The Wisdom of Swami Vivekananda: Insights and Inspiration from a Legendary Spiritual Teacher
54. Ayurvedic Remedies from the Garden
55. Sages and Seers
56. Rising Strong – Motivational Stories of Women
57. Beyond Flames -Mystery stories of Funeral Ghat Manikarnika
58. The Origins of Tulsi: A Look at the Mythological Roots of the Plant"

59. The Holistic Cow: A Look at the Physical, Spiritual, and Cultural Importance of Cows in India
60. Arts of Healing
61. Exploring the Divine
62. Understanding Five Elements
63. The Etymology of Ram
64. Symbols of India
65. Voice of Change (About Speeches of Great Men)
66. She Speaks (About Speeches of Great Women)
67. Patriotism on Celluloid – Brief About Patriotic Films
68. The Music of Motivation: A Brief Guide to Inspirational Film Songs
69. **Unlocking the Secrets of the Dashopanishads**
70. A Cultural Mosaic
71. Ancient Traditions, Modern Minds
72. Ecos of Ancient Wisdom
73. Beneath the Surface
74. From Temples to Ashrams
75. Sages of the Subcontinent
76. The Art of Healling (Ayurveda, Yoga & Naturopathy)
77. Indian Kitchen
78. The Festivals of India
79. The Indian Epics Retold
80. The Power of Mantras
81. The Indian River Ganges
82. The Indian Architecture
83. Rites of Passage
84. The Indian Silk Road
85. The Indian Literature
86. The Indian Villages
87. The Indian Folks & Crafts
88. The Way of Buddha
89. The Ramayan of Tulsidas

90. Astrological Remedies
91. The Secret Power of Motivation
92. Secret of Developing your Inner Strength
93. The Secret Path to Motivation
94. The Art and Secret of Positive Thinking
95. The Secrets of Practicing Ethical Living
96. Indian Art and Painting
97. The Indian Herbalism
98. Bharatanatyam to Kathak
99. Exploring India's Astrological Remedies

CONTACT

DR. JAGADEESH PILLAI

PhD in Vedic Science

Four Times Guinness World Record Holder

Winner of Mahatma Gandhi Vishwa Shanti Puraskar and Global Peace Ambassador

Gemology, Astro & Vastu Consultant - Spiritual Counselor

Consultant for designing World Record Ideas

Efficient Tarot Card Reader

9839093003

myrichindia@gmail.com

drjagadeeshpillai@facebook

drjagadeeshpillai@instagram

jagadeeshpillai@youtube

www. JAGADEESHPILLAI.com

|| LOKAHA SAMASTHAHA SUKHINO BHAVANTU ||

ഌ

Printed by Libri Plureos GmbH in Hamburg,
Germany